My First
Mazes

Illustrated by Isabel Aniel

Written by Elizabeth Golding

Designed by Anton Poitier & Ben Potter

BARRON'S

First edition for North America published in
2017 by Barron's Educational Series, Inc.

This book was conceived, created, and
produced by iSeek Ltd

Copyright © 2016 by iSeek Ltd
Written by: Elizabeth Golding
Illustrated by: Isabel Aniel
Designed by: Anton Poitier and Ben Potter

All inquiries should be addressed to:
Barron's Educational Series, Inc.
250 Wireless Boulevard
Hauppauge, New York 11788
www.barronseduc.com

ISBN: 978-1-4380-1003-8

Date of Manufacture: June 2017
Manufactured by: Grafo SA

Printed in Basauri, Spain

9 8 7 6 5 4 3

Be amazing!

This book is jam-packed with lots of fun mazes. Use a pencil to trace your way through each maze. It's best to have an eraser handy too, in case you go the wrong way and have to erase your way back!

Use your finger to trace the routes if you don't want to mark the book.

There is a question to answer on each page, too!

The mazes get a little harder toward the end. Don't worry if you get stuck with anything. The solutions are at the back of the book, but try not to peek!

Where did the king go?

He went to his c_____.

What did the boy catch?

He caught a b__.

How many friends did the frog find?

He found ☐ _ _ _ _ _ _ _ .

This elephant is scared of mice. Show him the way to the tree, and avoid the mice.

The elephant ate ⬜ apples on the way.

What did the monkey find?

He found a b_____.

What did the mouse eat?

She ate c_____.

What did the bears eat?

The bears ate h_____.

The fish is afraid of sharks.
Which way should he go?

The fish does not like s_____.

Which route should the dog choose to find his owners?

1   2

He chooses route

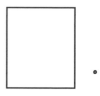

What did the children build?

They built a s___ c_____e.

Take the dark blue
car to the garage.

oes that blue car go over a bridge?

Yes ☐　　No ☐

Mole is lost! Which route takes him home?

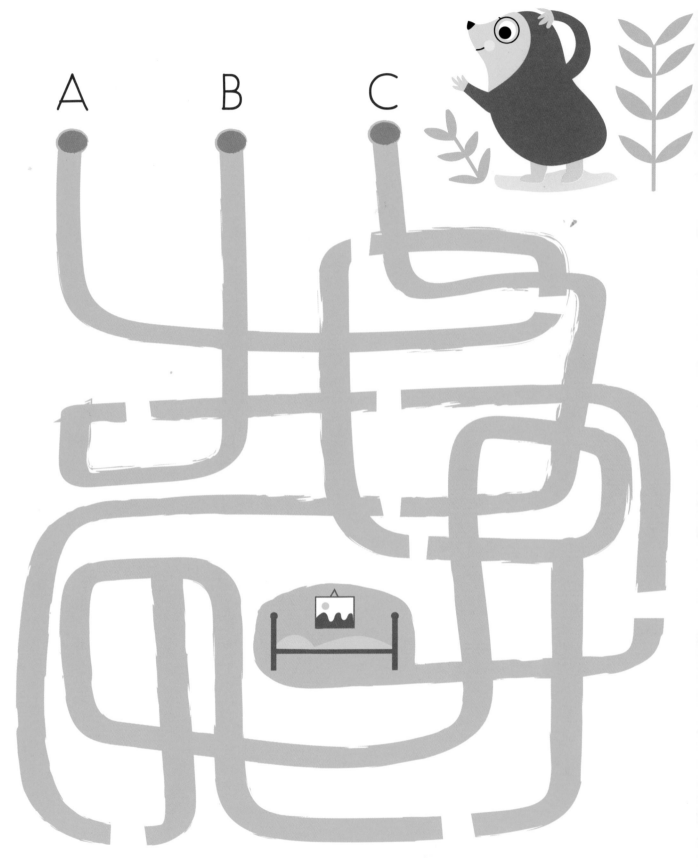

A   B   C

Mole chooses route _.

Where does the pig go?

He goes to the red ____.

The tiger wants to meet elephant. He is scared of hippos. Which way should he go?

Elephant met the t_____.

Avoid the cats to get the dog home!

The dog went to his d_____.

What does the pilot want to do?

He wants to fly his p_____.

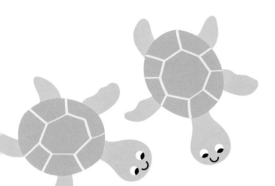

What color is the
turtles' friend?

He is b____.

How many friends does the red caterpillar have?

He has ⬚ friends.

The dog likes to eat things!
What is her favorite thing?

She likes b_____.

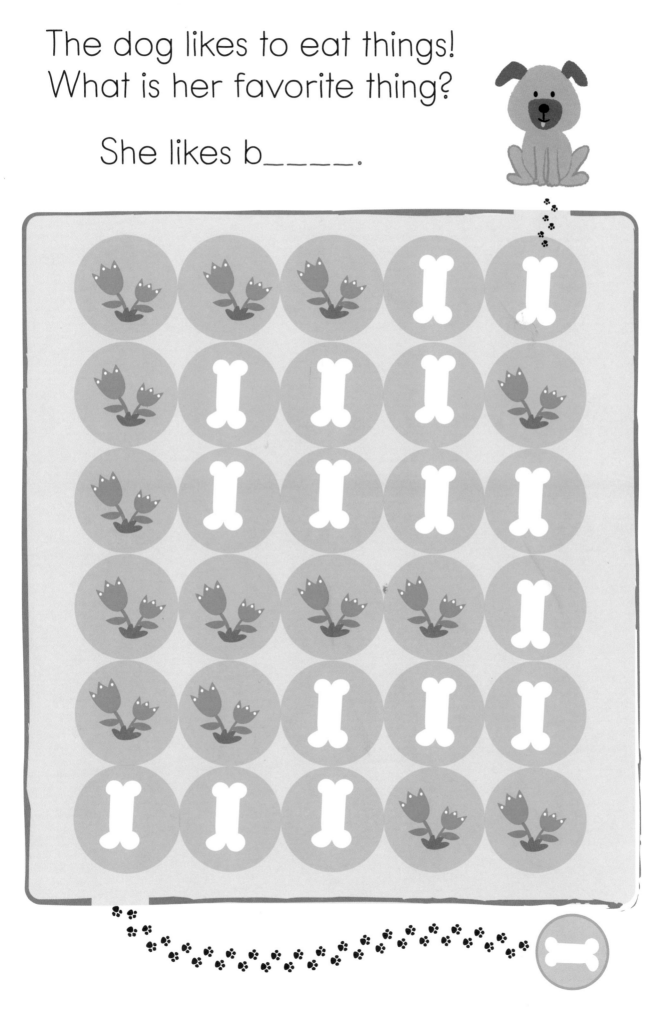

How many things do the rabbits eat?

They eat ☐ things.

What does the witch have in the haunted house?

She has a cauldron and a f____.

Get the cat to her basket by chasing the mice!

The cat likes her b_____.

Which rocket does the astronaut use?

The astronaut uses the g_____ rocket.

How many trees are on the ski slope?

There are ☐ trees.

Where does the princess go?

She goes to the c_____.

What is in the middle of the maze?

There is a b___ in the middle.

Avoid the dragons!
How many are in the maze?

There are ☐ dragons in the maze.

What does the baby find?

The baby finds a t_____.

Where does
the giraffe go?

She goes to
the t___.

What does the fish find?

He finds a f____.

Get from the straw to the cherry!

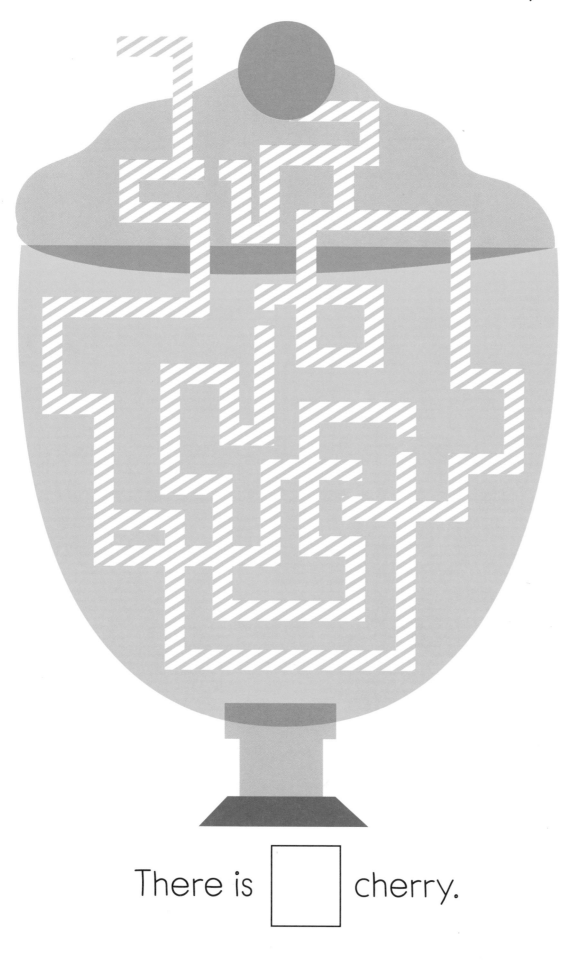

There is [ ] cherry.

Which route should the squirrel choose to find the acorn?

1   2   3

He should choose route ⬚.

Help the dogs find each other!

How many cats? There are ⬜ cats.

Help the penguins find each other.

I can see [ ] snowflakes.

What did the pirate find?

He found g_ _ _ _.

Get the elephant to the forest without passing a mouse!

There are ☐ trees in the forest.

Which rope
goes to the
anchor?

Rope
☐
goes
to the
anchor.

A

B

C

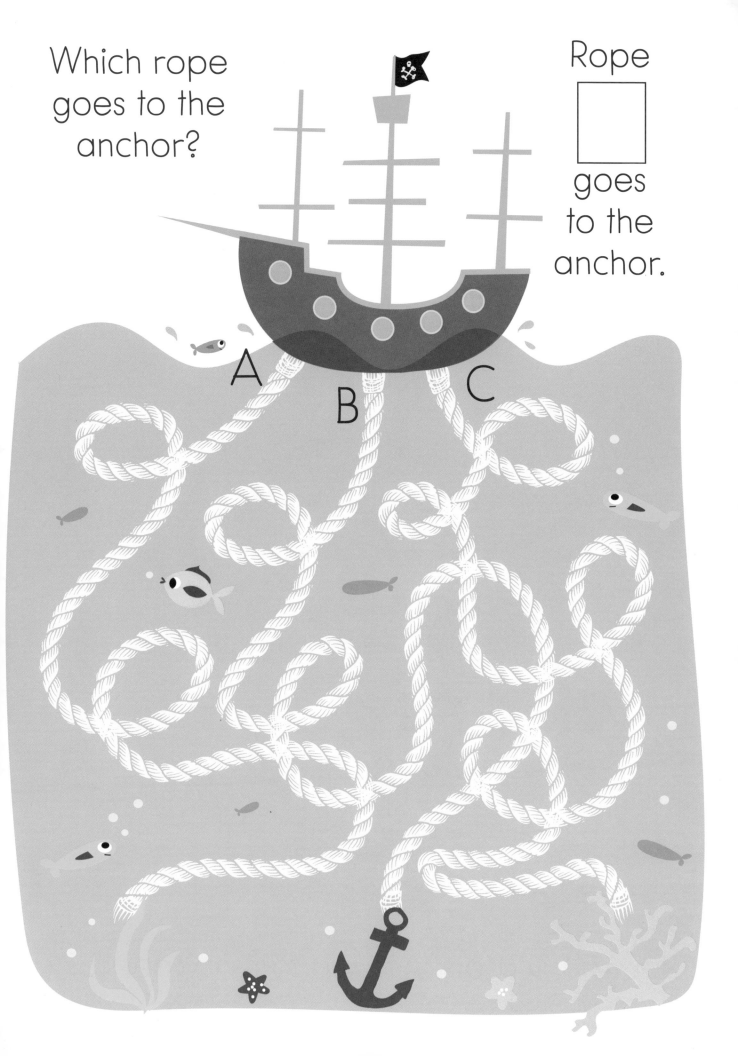

Which route
gets the dog
to its owner
fastest?

B

A

C

Route ☐ gets the dog to its owner fastest.

How many bears get to the woods?

[ ] bear(s) get(s) to the woods.

Which route does the bus take to park?

The bus takes route ☐ .

How many eggs
does the hen lay?

The hen lays ☐ eggs.

What does the polar bear catch?

The polar bear catches a f___.

Help the princess escape from the castle!

She escapes through the d___.

Get the boy home without meeting a monster! How many monsters can you see?

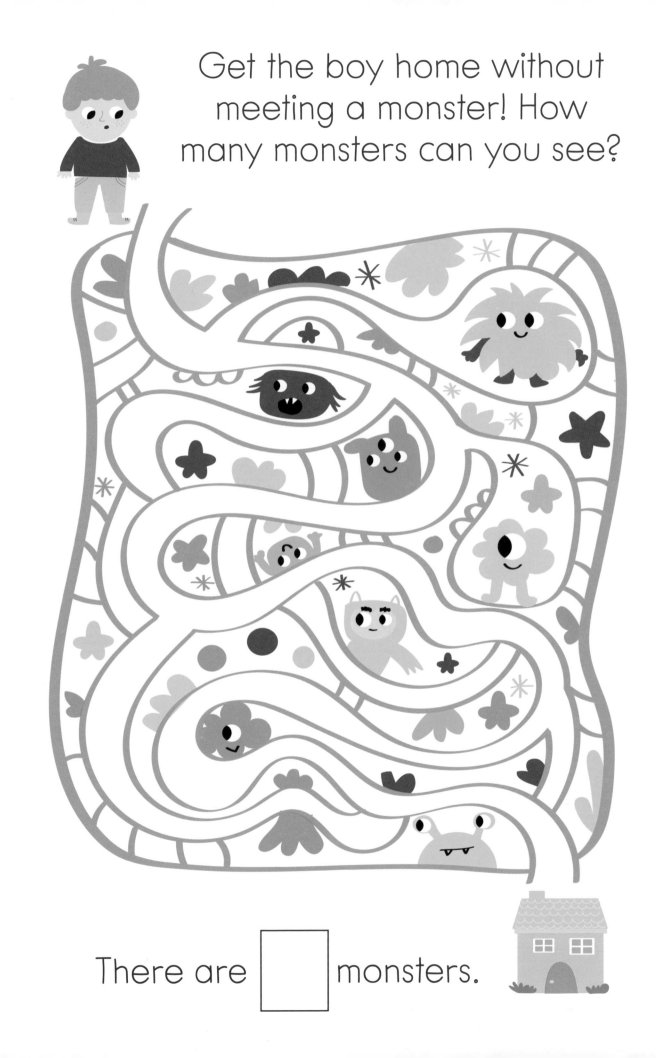

There are ☐ monsters.

Which route goes to the stables?

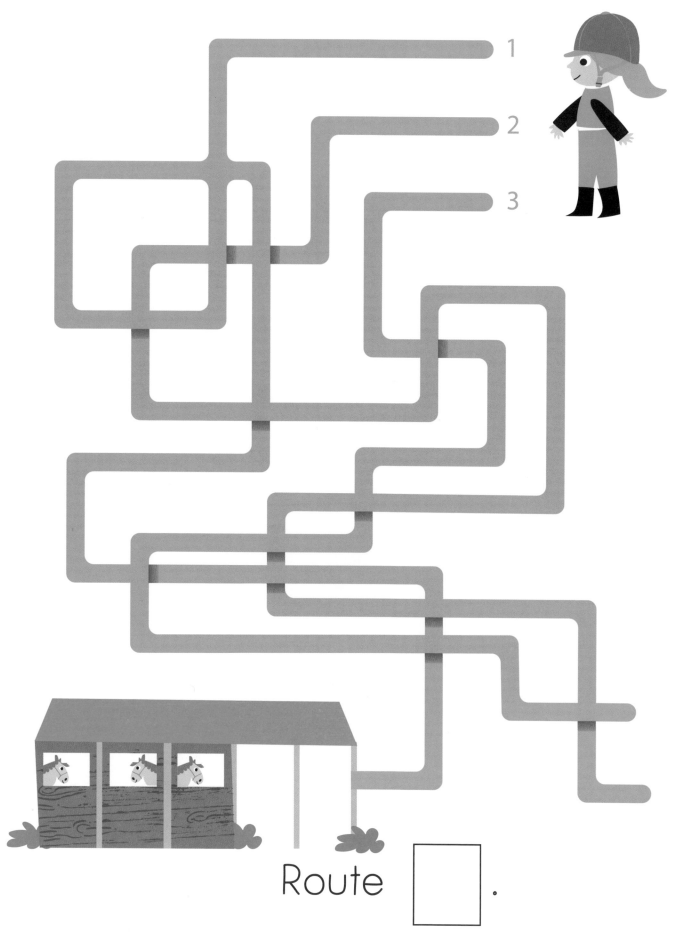

1

2

3

Route ☐.

Can the cat catch the mouse?

Yes ☐   No ☐

How many fish does the dolphin catch?

It catches fish.

Which route gets the man to the car?

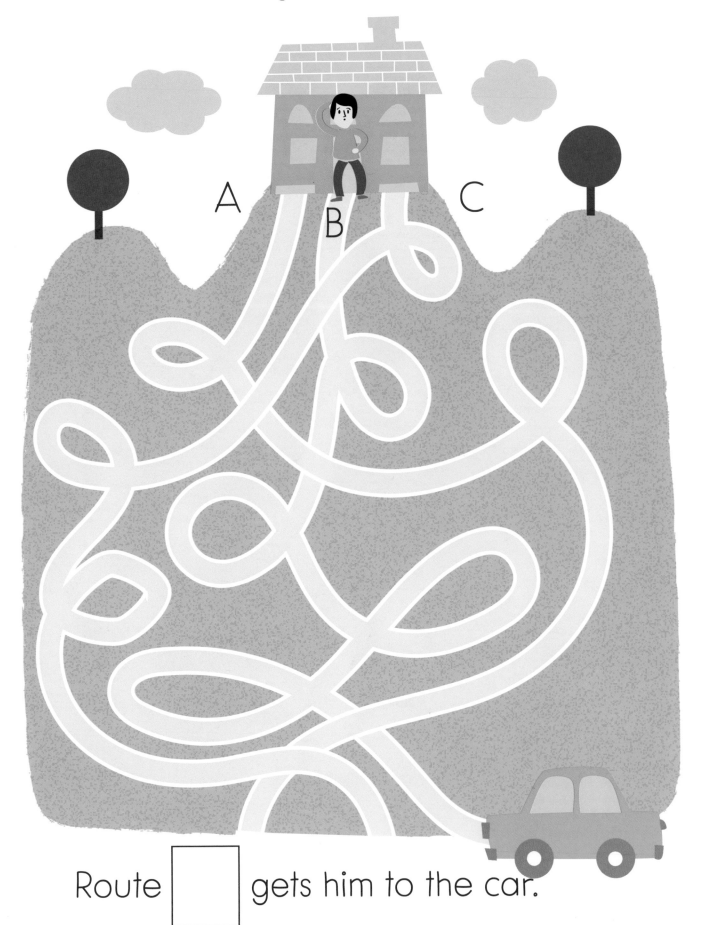

A   B   C

Route ☐ gets him to the car.

Which panda meets his friend fastest?

Panda [ ] meets his friend fastest.

Which route gets the lion to his cubs?

A

B

C

Route ☐ gets the lion to the cubs.

Which route gets the dog to the bone?

Route ⬜ gets the dog to the bone.

Which cat catches the mouse?

Cat ☐ catches the mouse.

Which route gets the children to the dog?

Route ☐ gets the children to the dog.

Which bee gets to the honey?

Bee ☐ gets the honey.

Take the bee to the middle of the flower.
How many yellow dots are on the flower?

There are ☐ yellow dots.

castle

bus

3 friends

cheese

honey

sharks

sand castle

c

barn

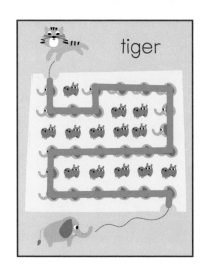
tiger

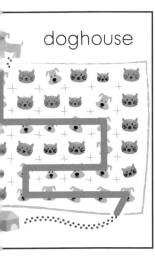
doghouse

plane

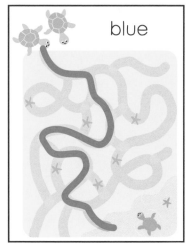
blue

3

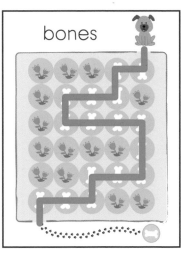
bones

3

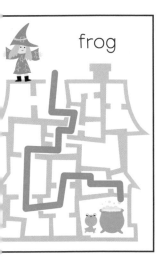
frog

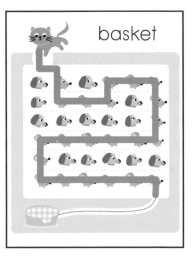
basket

green

3

castle

bird

5

teddy

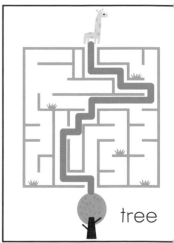

tree

frog

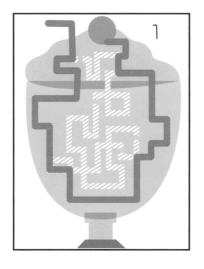

1

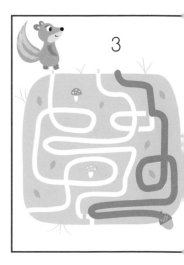

3

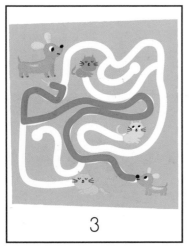

3

4

gold

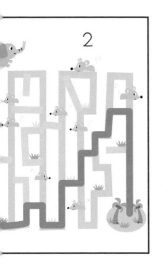

2

B

A

1

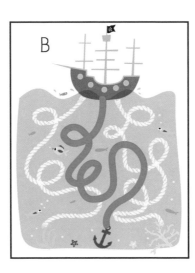

C

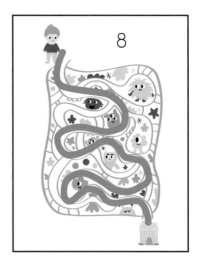

3

fish

door

8

Yes

4

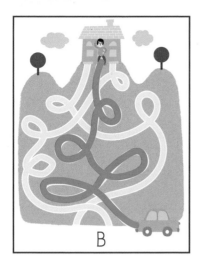

B

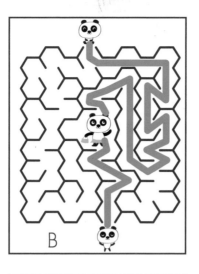

B

B

B

B

3

D

12